MW01154398

Antarctica

POLAR REGIONS BOOK WITH FACTS AND PICTURES FOR CHILDREN

The continent of Antarctica is one of the most remote and coldest places in the world. Its ice sheet is more than ninety percent thick, making the land an incredible place to explore.

This huge sheet contains over seventy percent of the world's fresh water and is home to a variety of marine life. However, the continent is devoid of any native people or permanent land mammals. Here are some fascinating facts about Antarctica for kids.

There are a number of interesting facts about Antarctica for kids. It is a unique continent, and children can learn about this amazing continent by reading books about it. These facts will help kids learn all they need to know about the frozen land.

These fun facts can also be used in school projects and other learning activities. If you are looking for a quick overview of Antarctica, here are some facts to get you started.

The harsh climate of Antarctica prevents most plants from growing. The climate is too cold to support any life. In fact, there are less than five species of plants, and most of them are bryophytes.

These lichens are the only vegetation to grow in the icy continent, and they only grow a few weeks each year. The only plants found in Antarctica are ferns and liverworts.

The most common animals that live in Antarctica are penguins and polar bears. They both live in the polar regions, but the southern hemisphere is a desert with zero rain.

Although Antarctica is the fifth largest continent in the world, it is a desert due to the lack of moisture. The water is 90% pure and has a low oxygen content. It is important to note that it is not a desert - the ice sheet is nearly a mile thick.

While Antarctica is largely land, it is covered in ice. A four-kilometer-thick ice sheet separates East Antarctica from West Antarctica.

The continent is divided into two parts by the Transantarctic Mountains. If you visit Antarctica, you will have the chance to see the South Pole. The ice sheet on the continent is home to the only ice-covered continent. Its polar reaches far beyond the arctic.

The climate of Antarctica is extremely cold and does not support plants. However, there are plants that grow in this region, despite the extreme conditions. While the climate of Antarctica is very cold, there is no sunlight.

The ice sheet is only two feet deep and contains no plants. The polar region is also covered with ice. While the ice sheet is the most pristine place on earth, it is the least populated continent.

The southernmost continent is unique in its landscape. It is full of ice and snow. The continent has no rain, making it a desert. Despite this, it is still covered with snow. In fact, 90% of the continent's surface is covered in ice.

Most of the people who visit this area of the world do so during the summer, when sea ice melts and temperatures become comfortable. Hence, it's best to visit Antarctica during the summer months.

There are many interesting facts about the continent. It is the only continent that doesn't have rain. Its ice sheet is covered with 90% of clean water. While Antarctica is not as inhabited as Alaska, it is still worth visiting.

Its ice sheet has a rich diversity of animals and is home to more than 100 species of mosses. Its ice sheet is nearly twice as large as Europe. Moreover, most of Antarctica is covered in ice that is over one mile thick. There are no rivers or lakes in the area, and the region is considered a desert.

Despite its extreme cold climate, Antarctica is home to many species of plants. There are over a hundred species of mosses and liverworts on the continent. But most of these plants are small and grow for a few weeks in the summer.

If you're planning to visit this area, make sure you plan ahead of time. You can plan an entire vacation around Antarctica. This unique and wonderful continent will fascinate your children and keep them occupied for years to come.

Lightning Source UK Ltd.
Milton Keynes UK
UKHW050838210223
417371UK00008B/121